PIANO SOLO

JURASSIC WORLD: FALLEN K...
MUSIC FROM THE MOTION PICTURE SOUNDTRACK

ISBN: 978-1-5400-3562-2

Visit Hal Leonard Online at
www.halleonard.com

Contact Us:
Hal Leonard
7777 West Bluemound Road
Milwaukee, WI 53213
Email: info@halleonard.com

In Europe contact:
Hal Leonard Europe Limited
Distribution Centre, Newmarket Road
Bury St Edmunds, Suffolk, IP33 3YB
Email: info@halleonardeurope.com

In Australia contact:
Hal Leonard Australia Pty. Ltd.
4 Lentara Court
Cheltenham, Victoria, 3192 Australia
Email: info@halleonard.com.au

CONTENTS

NOSTALGIA-SAURUS

By MICHAEL GIACCHINO

THE THERAPOD PRESERVATION SOCIETY

By MICHAEL GIACCHINO

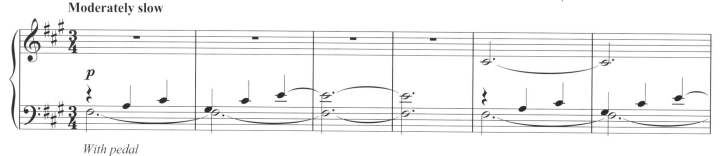

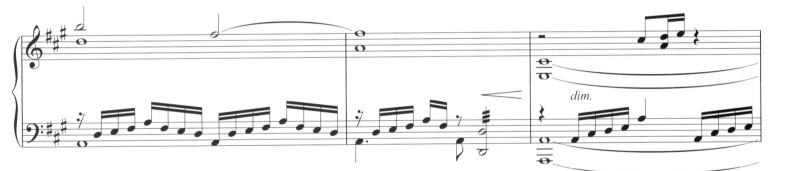

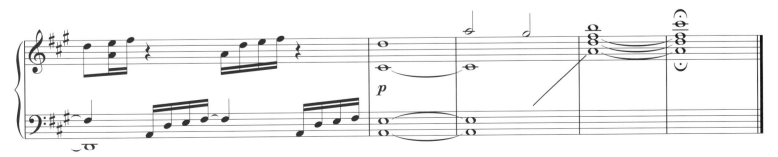

MAISIE AND THE ISLAND

By MICHAEL GIACCHINO

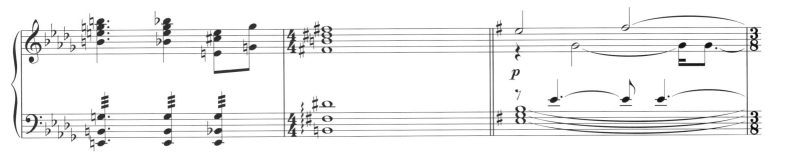

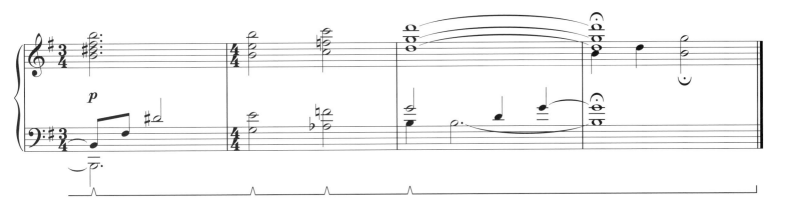

RAIDERS OF THE LOST ISLA NUBLAR

By MICHAEL GIACCHINO

Moderately, in 4

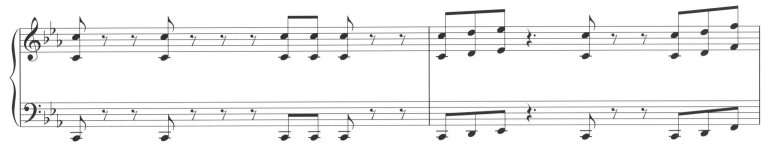

JURASSIC PILLOW TALK

By MICHAEL GIACCHINO

Moderately, in 2

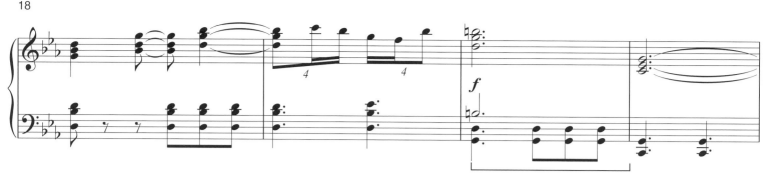

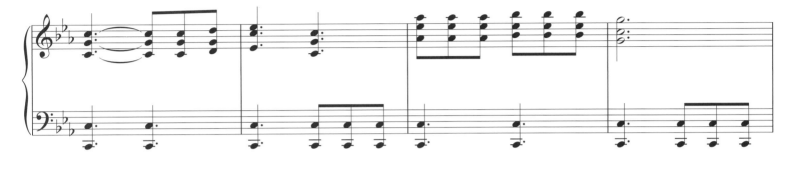

molto rit.

SHOCK AND AUCTION

By MICHAEL GIACCHINO

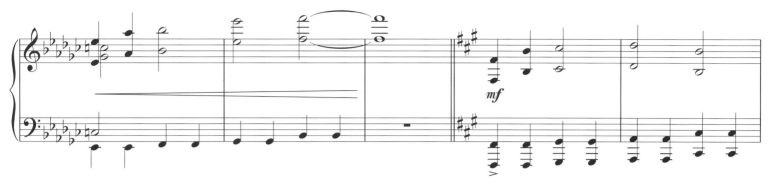

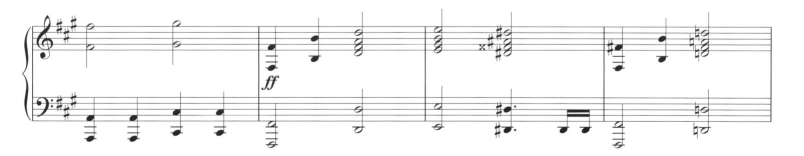

TO FREE OR NOT TO FREE

By MICHAEL GIACCHINO

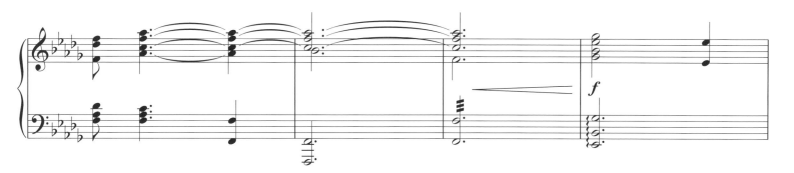

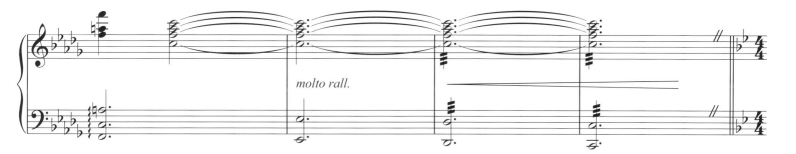

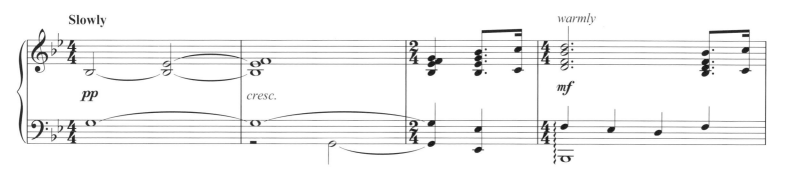

THE NEO-JURASSIC AGE

By MICHAEL GIACCHINO

Slowly and mysteriously

p

With pedal

mp

poco rit.

THUS BEGINS THE INDO-RAPTURE

By MICHAEL GIACCHINO

Slowly and dramatically

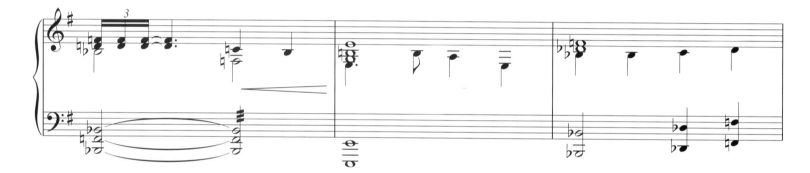

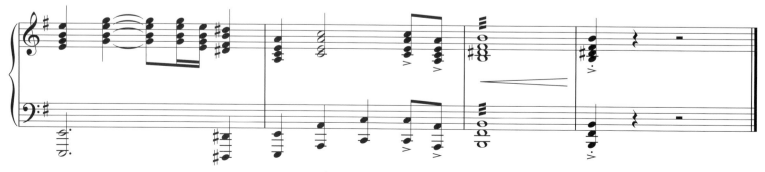

AT JURASSIC WORLD'S END CREDITS/SUITE

By MICHAEL GIACCHINO

Moderately slow, in 1

Pedal ad lib. throughout

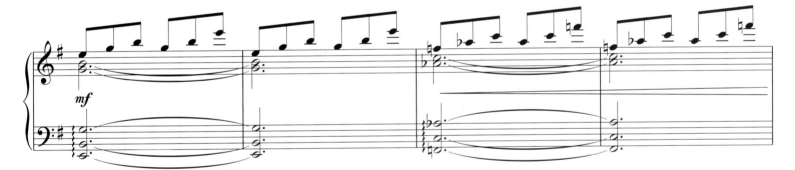

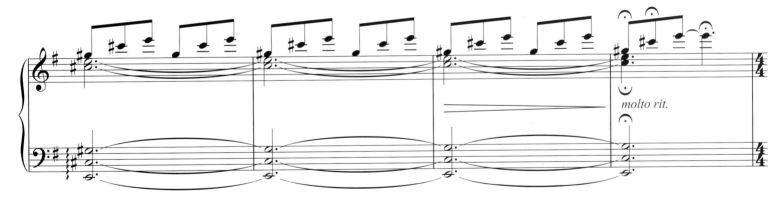

Slowly, expressively

Slightly faster

Very slowly, in 2

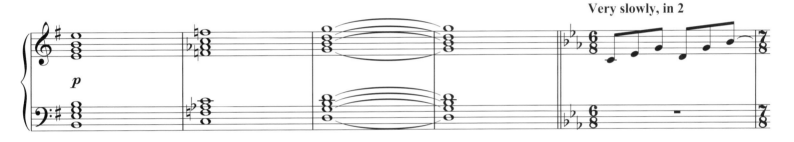

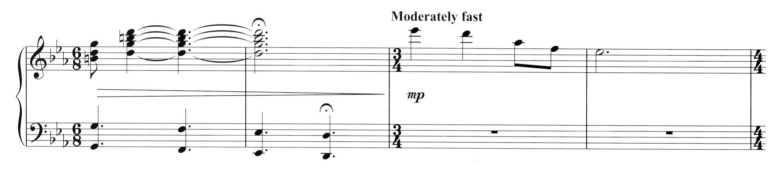

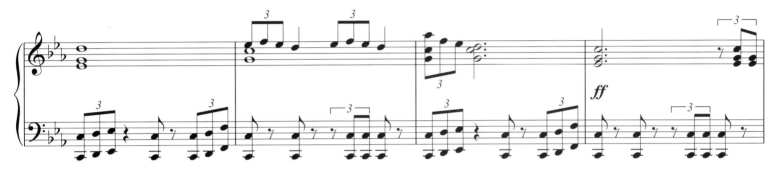

Slowly, in 1